making cushions

making cushions

Decorative projects for the home

Isabel Stanley
Photography by Mark Wood and Adrian Taylor

southwater

This edition is published by Southwater

Southwater is an imprint of
Anness Publishing Limited
Hermes House
88–89 Blackfriars Road
London SE1 8HA
tel. 020 7401 2077
fax 020 7633 9499

Distributed in the UK by
The Manning Partnership
251–253 London Road East
Batheaston
Bath BA1 7RL
tel. 01225 852 727
fax 01225 852 852

Distributed in the USA by
Anness Publishing Inc.
27 West 20th Street
Suite 504
New York
NY 10011
tel. 212 807 6739
fax 212 807 6813

Distributed in Australia by
Sandstone Publishing
Unit 1
360 Norton Street
Leichhardt
New South Wales 2040
tel. 02 9560 7888
fax 02 9560 7488

1 3 5 7 9 10 8 6 4 2

Publisher: Joanna Lorenz
Senior Editor: Clare Nicholson
Designer: Bobbie Colgate Stone
Stylists: Fanny Ward, Deena Beverly and Jenny Norton
Photography: Adrian Taylor and Mark Wood
Step-by-step Photography: Lucy Tizard

MEASUREMENTS
Both imperial and metric measurements have been given in the text. Where conversions produce an
awkward number, these have been rounded for convenience, but will produce an accurate result if one
system is used throughout.

Previously published as *Inspirations: Cushions*

CONTENTS

INTRODUCTION

THERE IS something luxurious, even indulgent, about cushions, because they exist only to make life more comfortable. They have a place in every room and, as long as they are not used too often for pillow fights, they will last for years and become old favorites with you and your family.

Besides the comfort that they provide, cushions can help you instantly transform your home by adding decorative detail to any interior. Use them to make dramatic changes to the feel of a sofa or the color scheme of a room, simply by adding bright primary hues or soft neutral ones. A cushion can soften the hard seat of a dining-room chair or serve as the perfect stylish gift for a friend. Tuck a bolster behind your head as you curl up to read a book, or throw a pillow in the back of the car to serve as an outdoor seat when you go on a picnic.

Inspirations: Cushions clearly demonstrates, using step-by-step photography, how to make a wide selection of soft furnishings. There are sections covering the materials, equipment and basic techniques that you may need to attempt the projects featured. Take your inspiration from the designs, which range from basic cushions made from dish towels to elaborate monogrammed *objets d'art*.

Do not restrict your endeavors to the standard square: Cushions can be small, large, round or a bolster. Fabrics can be kept simple, or, alternatively, you could use a piece of antique tapestry or expensive brocade that you have been saving for a long time. You can leave the edges plain, or trim them with braid or decorative frills. Mix colors and patterns, add surface details, and create your own individual selection.

Deborah Barker

EMBROIDERED HEART

Warm wool blanketing and vibrant colors give this cushion a homespun Shaker appeal, and you can add as much or as little embroidery as you like to make it truly personal. The colorful pom-poms made with several strands of tapestry yarn are extra speedy.

YOU WILL NEED
12-inch square of gray blanket
vanishing fabric marker
small piece of pink blanket
scrap fabric
fabric glue
tapestry needle
tapestry yarn
cotton fabric for backing
two pieces of blanket in contrasting colors
thread
cardboard
Velcro
12-inch square cushion pad

1 Trace the heart template from the back of the book and cut it out. Place the template in the center of the gray square and draw around it with the vanishing fabric marker.

2 Cut out the heart. Place the template on the pink blanket, draw around it and cut it out.

3 Place the pink heart in the cut-out area of the gray blanket, and glue a piece of scrap fabric behind the heart to hold it in place. Let dry.

4 Using the tapestry needle and yarn, work a straight stitch around the edge of the heart.

5 Embroider the heart with colorful cross-stitches in tapestry yarn.

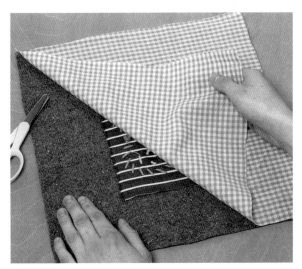

6 Cut a piece of backing fabric 12 inches square and place it on the back of the blanket appliqué.

7 Cut two cushion back pieces, each 12 x 8 inches, and embellish the edge of each piece with a running stitch in a contrasting color of thread (hem the edge first if not cut on a blanket selvage). Place the two cushion backs on the cushion front, with right sides facing and back pieces overlapping. Baste in place. Machine-stitch around the square with a ½-inch seam allowance. Turn the cover right side out, and press. Remove any visible basting thread. ▶

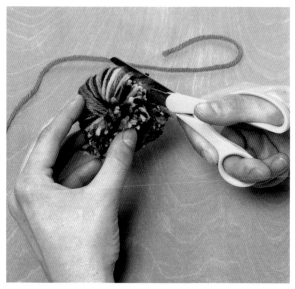

8 To make a pom-pom, cut two 2-inch-diameter cardboard rings with a 1-inch hole in the center. Knot strands of tapestry yarn onto the pieces of cardboard and wrap the yarn around until the hole is full.

9 Insert the blade of a pair of scissors between the cardboard rings and cut the yarn. Tie a 12-inch length of yarn between the cardboard rings and tie in a knot. Remove the cardboard and fluff up the pom-pom.

10 Make three more pom-poms the same size and sew one to each corner of the cushion. Sew a small piece of Velcro to the two opening edges of the cover. Insert the cushion pad and close the fastening.

SCALLOPS AND BUTTONS

Bring some color to your couch with this vibrant scallop-edged cushion. Ours is made in fine-wale corduroy, but you could use any closely woven fabric. Add embroidered self-covered buttons, or simply use large colored buttons if you want to save time.

YOU WILL NEED
12 inches of 36-inch-wide fine-wale corduroy in each of three
different colors
cord
masking tape
thread
cotton embroidery floss
pinking shears
scraps of fabric for covering buttons
three self-covered buttons
button maker (optional)
16 x 10-inch cushion pad

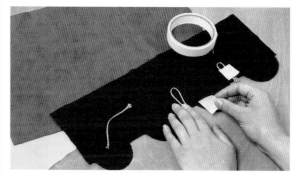

1 Trace the scalloped pattern piece from the back of the book. From the corduroy, cut one back 16½ x 11 inches and one front measuring 16½ x 10 inches. Using the scalloped pattern piece, cut two pieces for the border. Cut three 4½-inch lengths of cord and make each one into a loop. Place each loop in between the scallops, with the ends of the cord meeting the raw fabric edge. Secure them with masking tape.

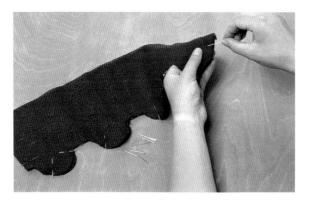

2 Place the two scallop-edged pieces of fabric together with right sides facing, and sew along the scalloped edge with a ½-inch seam allowance.

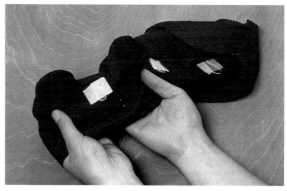

3 Turn right side out and remove the masking tape. Press the fabric well.

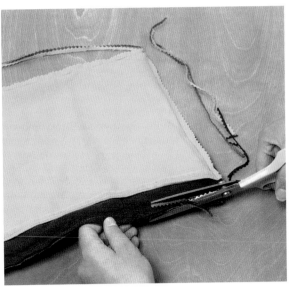

4 Hand-sew a running stitch along the scalloped edge in a contrasting color of embroidery floss. Make a narrow double hem on one long side of the cushion front.

5 Take the pieces of fabric for the cushion front and back. Place the scalloped front on the cushion back with right sides facing, then place the hemmed cushion front on top, right side down. Baste, then machine-stitch the edge with a ½-inch seam allowance. Snip the corners and trim the seams with pinking shears. Turn right side out and press.

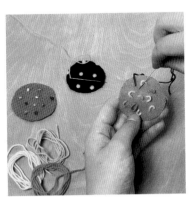

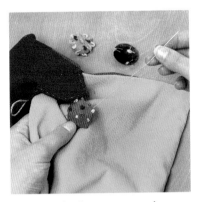

6 Cut three circles of fabric in different colors, ¼ inch larger than the buttons. Embellish each one with some embroidery stitches.

7 Cover each button using a button maker, or simply sew a running stitch around the edge of each circle and pull up the thread to gather the fabric. Press the button backs into position.

8 Sew the buttons onto the cover to correspond with the cord loops. Insert the cushion pad and then fasten the loops.

GOING DOTTY

Have fun creating your own polka-dotted fabric design with fabric paints. Stick to just two or three complementary colors, or go for a jazzy, multicolored effect. If you are nervous about painting the dots freehand, practice making them first on scrap paper.

YOU WILL NEED

16 inches of 36-inch-wide
white linen
12 inches of 36-inch-wide
colored linen
thread
fabric paints
small paintbrush
cotton embroidery floss
selection of buttons
contrasting fabric for the piping
2 yards piping cord
Velcro

1 Cut out two pieces of white linen: a 16-inch square for the front and a 16½ x 9-inch rectangle for the back. From the colored linen, cut a 16½ x 12-inch rectangle for the back. Fold over ½ inch of one edge of each back piece to make a hem, and stitch in place.

2 Place the front of the cushion on a flat, covered surface and paint on different-colored dots using fabric paints and the small paintbrush. Let dry.

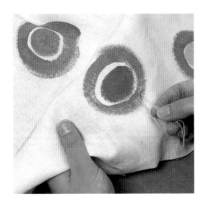

3 Decorate the dots with circles of running stitches in contrasting embroidery floss.

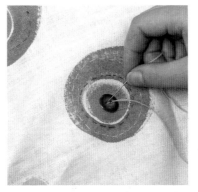

4 Sew a button in the center of each of the dots.

5 Work a line of running stitch along the hem of the white cushion back.

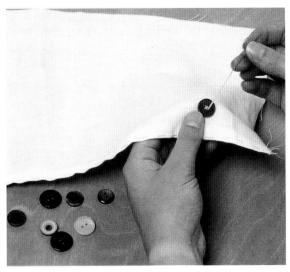

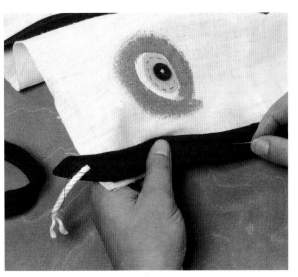

6 Sew a line of different-shaped and -colored buttons above the running stitch. For the piping, cut 1½-inch-wide bias strips of fabric and join them to make a 2-yard-long strip. Fold this strip in half over the piping cord and stitch in place.

7 Pin the piping around the edge of the cushion front with raw edges matching, and baste. Place the cushion backs on the cushion front with right sides facing. Using a zipper foot on the sewing machine, stitch the edges of the cushion close to the piping.

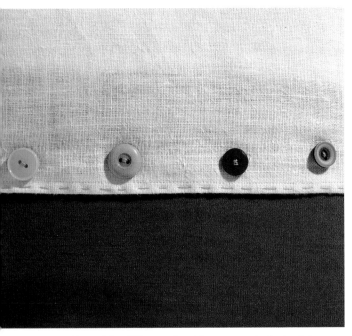

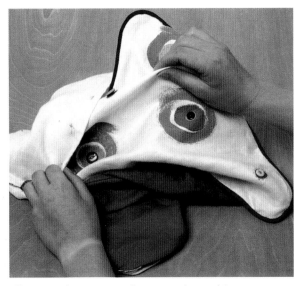

Above: The different-colored buttons on the back of the cushion continue the polka-dot theme.

8 Snip the corners, then turn the cushion cover right side out and press. Sew a small piece of Velcro to the two opening edges of the cushion cover. Insert the cushion pad and close the fastening.

TEA-TIME APPLIQUÉ

Combine attractive appliqué cups and saucers with linen dish towels to create a simple cushion for a kitchen chair. Linen dish towels come in a range of colors, so you can match the appliqué to suit your own color scheme.

YOU WILL NEED
2 linen dish towels
fusible bonding web
scraps of blue fabric in different patterns
embroidery floss
thread
¾-inch self-covered buttons
button maker (optional)
16 x 10-inch cushion pad

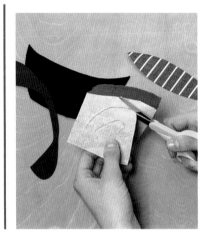

1 From the dish towels, cut a front piece measuring 14½ x 16½ inches, and two back pieces measuring 10 x 16½ inches and 11 x 16½ inches. Iron the bonding web onto the back of the scraps of blue fabric. Trace the templates from the back of the book, and draw around them onto the bonding web. Cut out the teacup shapes.

2 Peel the backing paper from the bonding web, position the shapes on the front of the cushion fabric and iron in place.

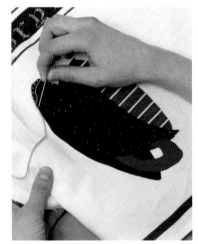

3 Embellish the cup and saucer with an assortment of simple stitches (see Techniques), using embroidery floss.

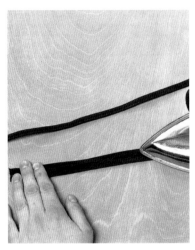

4 Cut a strip of fabric 22 x 1½ inches. Fold the strip in half horizontally and press. Open out the fabric, fold the two sides into the center and press, then fold in half.

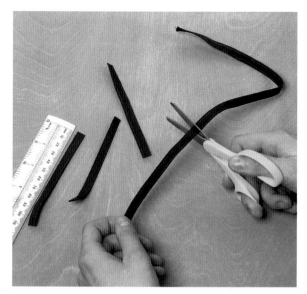

5 Sew along each side of the strip, then cut the strip into five 4½-inch lengths.

6 Fold each length in half to make a loop, and press. Position the loops along the long edge of one of the back pieces, on the wrong side. Baste in place and then stitch along the hem line.

7 Place the back piece with the loops on top of the appliqué, with right sides facing, then place the second piece on top. Baste and machine-stitch around the edge with a ½-inch seam. Snip the corners, turn right side out and press. Remove the basting thread.

8 To cover the buttons, cut five circles of blue fabric from the remaining scraps.

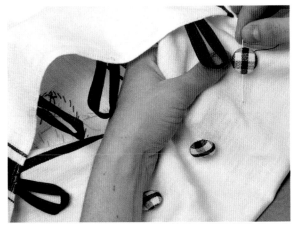

9 Cover each button using a button maker, or simply sew a running stitch around the edge of the circle and pull up the thread to gather the fabric. Press the backs of the buttons into position.

10 Sew the buttons on the back of the cushion to correspond with the button loops. Insert the cushion pad and fasten the loops.

Right: The simple gingham buttons complete the country look of this kitchen cushion.

NAUTICAL NOTE

Blue-and-white stripes and rope are two classic nautical themes – ideal for a bathroom or for a fresh seaside-inspired color scheme. Our cushion is round, but the rope idea would work just as well on a square or rectangular cushion.

YOU WILL NEED
large sheet of paper
thread
pushpin
pencil
24 inches of 54-inch-wide striped canvas
tailor's chalk
twelve ½-inch eyelets and tool
hammer
18-inch-diameter cushion pad
2¼ yards of ½-inch rope
strong off-white thread
Velcro

1 Draw a 21-inch-diameter circle on paper using thread, a pushpin and a pencil. Cut out.

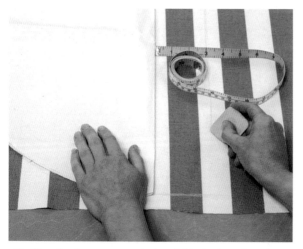

2 For the front, cut a circle of fabric, keeping the stripes equal on each side of the center. For the back pieces, place the folded pattern on the fabric so that the stripes match the front piece. Add 3 inches to the straight edge and cut out, then repeat.

3 Fold under and baste a 1-inch hem along the straight edges of the back pieces. Stitch close to the hem edge and then topstitch. Overlap the two pieces to make a circle the same size as the front panel, and baste together along the straight edges. ▶

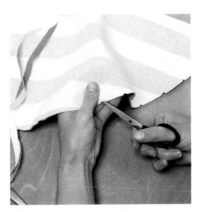

4 With right sides facing, pin the back and front together, matching the stripes. Baste into position, then machine-stitch with a ½-inch seam allowance. Remove the basting thread.

5 Trim the seam allowance to ¼ inch. Snip notches around the edge and turn the cover right side out. Roll the seam between your fingers and baste close to the edge. Topstitch around the cover, 1 inch from the edge.

6 Fold the cover in fourths and, using tailor's chalk, mark the position of an eyelet in the middle of the border at each fold. Mark the positions of the other eyelets at equal intervals. Follow the manufacturer's instructions to insert an eyelet at each mark.

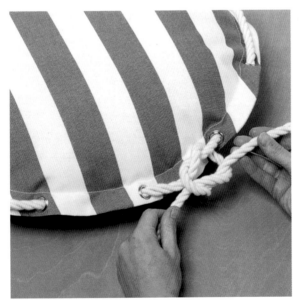

7 Insert the cushion pad and, beginning on the right side, thread the rope through the eyelets. Tie a reef knot by taking the left rope over the right rope and under, then the right rope over the left and under.

8 Whip the ends of the rope with the strong thread and sew in the ends securely. Cut the rope close to the whipping to finish. Sew a piece of Velcro to the overlapping edges on the back of the cushion cover.

FLOWER POWER

Big, bold, colorful flowers give this cushion a childlike simplicity. This is an ideal cushion for a beginner, as it is a simple square shape and the flowers are cut from a template. The self-covered buttons are easy to make, yet give a professional-looking finish.

YOU WILL NEED
blanket in two contrasting colors
tapestry needle
crewel yarn
thread
scraps of blanket
scraps of fine wool fabric
1¼-inch self-covered buttons
button maker (optional)
Velcro
24-inch-square cushion pad

1 Measure and cut out three pieces of blanket: a 24-inch square for the front, and two 24 x 16-inch pieces for the back. Embellish the edges of the cushion backs with a running stitch in a contrasting-colored crewel yarn (hem the edges first if not cut on a blanket selvage).

2 Place the two back pieces of blanket on the cushion front, with right sides facing. Pin in place and sew together around the edge with a ½-inch seam allowance. Snip the corners, turn the cover right side out and press.

3 Work a blanket stitch (see Techniques) around the edge of the cushion, using a different-colored crewel yarn for each side.

4 Trace the flower template from the back of the book. Draw around it, and cut out nine flowers from the scraps of blanket.

5 Position the flowers on the blanket square in a grid, and pin them in place.

6 Cut nine circles of colored fine wool fabric to cover the buttons.

7 Cover the buttons (see Step 7 on page 14), and press the backs of the buttons into position.

8 Sew a button to the center of each flower. Sew a small piece of Velcro to the opening edges of the cushion. Insert the cushion pad and close the fastening.

PATCHWORK VELVET PINCUSHION

In Victorian times, pincushions were sewn to commemorate births, christenings, weddings and Valentine's Day. This small patchwork of velvets, trimmed with gold braid and decorated with brass pins, would make a lovely gift for anyone who likes to sew.

YOU WILL NEED
scraps of velvet in yellow, pink, green and brown
thread
polyester stuffing
narrow gold braid
brass lace-making pins
four yellow ribbon roses
fray-resistant glue
fabric glue
small gold beads

1 From velvet, cut one 4-inch yellow square, four 3-inch pink squares and four 3 x 4-inch green rectangles. With right sides facing and with a ½-inch seam allowance, sew the pieces into three strips: join a pink square to each of the short ends of the two green rectangles, and stitch the other two green rectangles to opposite sides of the yellow square.

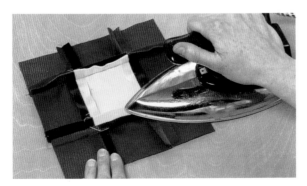

2 Press the seams open, then pin and stitch one narrow strip to either side of the wide strip. Do not worry if the seams are not precisely accurate, as they will be covered by the gold braid. Press the two long seams open.

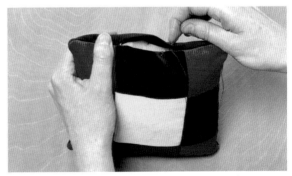

3 Cut an 8-inch square of brown velvet, and pin it to the patchwork square with right sides facing. Seam around the outside edge, leaving a gap of about 2 inches on one side. Clip the corners, turn right side out and fill with stuffing. Close the opening with a slip stitch.

4 Attach gold braid around the center square with brass pins, mitering the corners (see Techniques).

5 Pin a yellow ribbon rose to each corner of the center square.

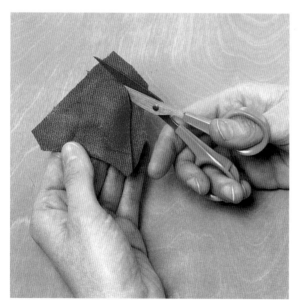

6 Trace the heart template from the back of the book onto thin paper, and cut it out. Draw around the heart on the wrong side of a piece of pink velvet, and coat the pencil line with a thin layer of fray-resistant glue. Let dry, then cut out.

7 Attach the heart to the center square with a light layer of fabric glue. When this is dry, use brass pins to attach small gold beads all the way around the outside edge of the heart.

CARPE DIEM

"Carpe diem" means literally "seize the day." You may feel slightly guilty as you recline on the sofa with this invigorating motto, but do not worry. Help yourself to another chocolate and resolve to seize the day tomorrow.

YOU WILL NEED
20 inches of 45-inch-wide linen, prewashed
soft pencil
masking tape
embroidery hoop
embroidery needle
embroidery floss in mushroom brown
2¼ yards of ½-inch antique-gold flat braid
12 x 16-inch cushion pad

1 Cut a piece of fabric measuring 13 x 17 inches for the cushion front. Trace the template from the back of the book. Using a soft pencil, draw thickly over the lines of the motto on the reverse side of the tracing paper.

2 Position the tracing centrally on the front piece of linen, and secure it with masking tape. Draw over the outline to transfer the design to the fabric.

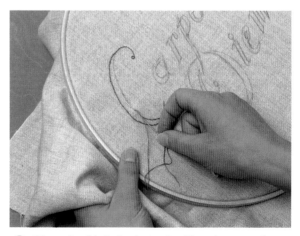

3 Place the fabric in the embroidery hoop, and then embroider a clear outline for each letter using a backstitch.

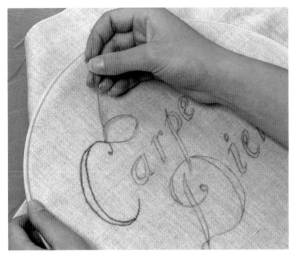

4 To emphasize the scrolled parts of each letter, whip the backstitch, passing around the backstitches only (not through the fabric beneath).

5 Fill in the solid parts of the letters, using long and short stitches worked in a vertical direction within each letter.

6 Work a satin stitch across each letter, forming a smooth, slightly padded horizontal surface that covers the long and short stitches. Take care gradually to adjust the angle of the satin stitch as you follow the curves of each letter, to produce a flowing, scriptlike form.

7 To make up the cushion cover, cut two back pieces measuring 13 x 11 inches. Make a narrow double hem on one long edge of each back piece. Overlap the back pieces, and pin them to the cushion front with right sides facing and raw edges matching. Machine-stitch, making a ½-inch seam.

For the border, cut two strips measuring 9 x 22½ inches. Fold each border strip in half lengthwise and, starting ½ inch from the edge of the fold, draw a line at a 45° angle to the raw edges of the strip. Unfold and pin the four border pieces together along the marked lines to make a rectangle. Stitch seams. Trim the seam allowances to ½ inch. Press seams open and turn the border right side out.

With right sides together, pin the back edge of the border to the back of the cushion cover, matching raw edges and corners. Baste, then machine-stitch in place, pivoting the work on the needle at the corners. Press turnings toward the border.

Fold the border in half and pin the front edge to the cushion front. Slip-stitch in place, through the first line of stitching. Pin the flat braid over the slip stitching and hand-sew in place, folding the braid neatly at the corners to form miters. Insert the cushion pad.

TAKE A SEAT

Make a ribbon-trimmed seat cushion for a favorite chair. Match the color of the fabric and ribbons to your tablecloth or patio umbrella to create a coordinating set. If you want a more fitted cushion, make a paper pattern of your chair seat and use it to cut out the fabric.

YOU WILL NEED
32 inches of 54-inch-wide fabric
8 ounces polyester batting
thread
vanishing fabric marker
5½ yards each of ⅛-inch embroidery ribbon in six different shades
(blues, greens and yellows)
large needle
3-inch square of stiff cardboard
two ½-inch wooden beads

1 Cut two 18-inch squares of fabric and batting, and place a fabric square on top of each batting square. Work lines of basting thread, radiating out from the center, to hold the two layers together.

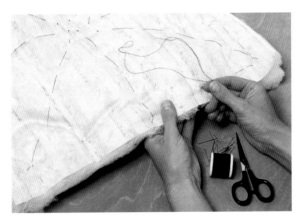

2 Pin the two panels together with the batting inside, and baste securely around each side 1 inch from the edge.

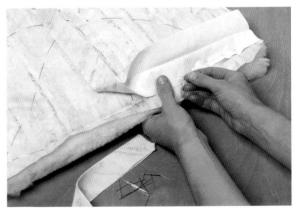

3 Cut four 3-inch-wide bias strips, about 20 inches long, from the remaining fabric, and press to remove some of the stretch. Press in half lengthwise. Pin, baste and stitch the bias strips along the edges of the cushion, keeping the edge of each strip along the basted line.

3 4

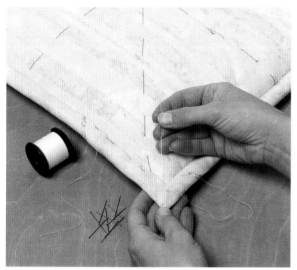

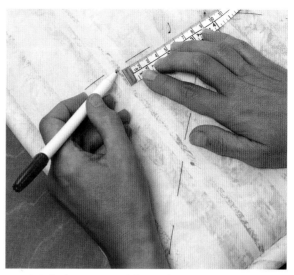

4 Trim the batting and fabric to the edge of the binding. Fold the binding to the back, turn it under and pin. Miter the corners and trim away any excess fabric before slip stitching. Slip-stitch the rest of the binding. Remove any visible basting thread.

5 Mark the center of the cushion on the right side with the vanishing fabric marker, and then measure out from the center to make a grid of nine marks, each 4 inches apart.

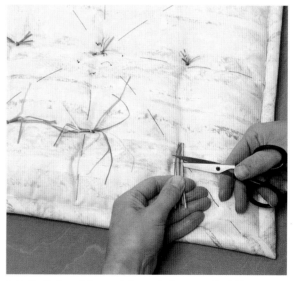

6 Thread 8-inch lengths of ribbon onto a needle. Insert the needle through the cushion at one of the marks, leaving 2 inches of ends on the right side. Bring the needle back up and go through the same holes, leaving the ends on the right side.

7 Pull the ribbons tight and tie securely. Trim the ends to ¾ inch. Repeat at the other eight marks.

8 Wrap all six colors of ribbon around the stiff cardboard six times. Cut the ends, then thread a single length of ribbon underneath the ribbons and tie securely. Snip the ribbons off the cardboard and press to remove the creases.

9 Place a wooden bead under the tie and pull the ribbons down to cover it. Tie a second length of single ribbon around the ribbons to form the neck of the tassel, and tie securely. Trim the ends neatly. Make another tassel to match, and stitch them onto the front corners of the cushion.

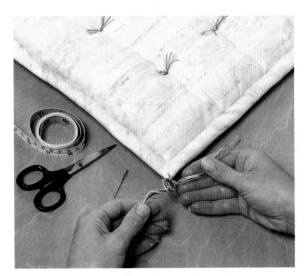

10 Cut two bundles of 12-inch lengths of ribbon. Wrap a single length of ribbon around the center of each bundle to hold the ribbons in place. Stitch these central ribbons to the back corners of the cushion and knot the ribbons. Tie the ribbons around the back of the chair.

Above: A more fitted cushion is just as easy to make, and looks very stylish on a simple kitchen chair.

FRINGED VELVET

Do you have a collection of fabric remnants and trimmings hidden away in a cupboard? If so, bring them out and transform them into a sumptuous patchwork cushion that will grace any sofa. Try notions departments as sources of beautiful fringes and trimmings.

YOU WILL NEED
20 inches of 36-inch-wide velvet for cushion back
thread
16-inch zipper
cardboard
16-inch square each of red, gray and green velvet
pinking shears
32-inch beaded fringe
24 x 16-inch cushion pad

1 For the cushion back, cut one piece of velvet 17 x 3¼ inches and one piece measuring 23 x 17 inches. Join the two pieces, inserting a zipper in the center of the seam (see Techniques). Make a cardboard template for a triangle from the back of the book. Cut out a triangle from red velvet, using pinking shears. Cut out a gray velvet triangle in the same way, then turn the template over and cut out another gray and red triangle. Cut two green velvet triangles, then turn the template over and cut out two more. Pin a green and a red triangle right sides together along the diagonal edges. Machine-stitch with a ¼-inch seam and repeat for the three other pairs of triangles.

2 Pin two patched rectangles right sides facing along their longest edges, matching diagonal seams. Machine-stitch with a ½-inch seam.

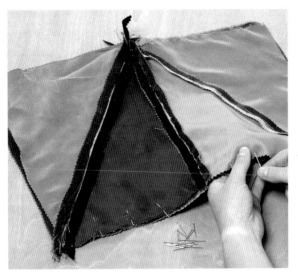

3 Pin the two front halves of the cushion together, carefully matching the center seams, and machine-stitch with a ½-inch seam.

4 Press the seams open, and trim down the seam allowances to reduce the bulk of fabric.

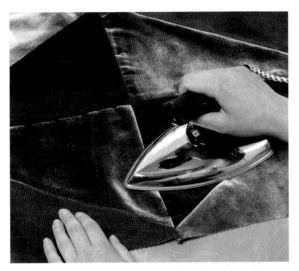

5 Lightly press the seams on the right side of the patchwork using a cool iron.

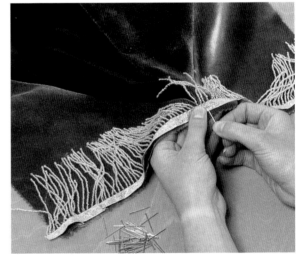

6 Cut two 16-inch lengths of fringing, and pin one to each short edge of the cushion front. Machine-stitch in place, using a zipper foot to avoid breaking the beads. With the zipper open and right sides facing, pin and machine-stitch the cushion front and back together with a ½-inch seam. Clip the corners and turn the cover right side out. Insert the cushion pad and close the zipper.

PERSONALLY YOURS

Perfect as a christening gift or to celebrate the birth of a baby, this delicate cushion in fresh gingham and broderie anglaise has timeless appeal. Photocopy your chosen initials – calligraphy books are always a good source of attractive lettering – so they are ready to transfer to the fabric.

YOU WILL NEED
5-inch square of 12-count
Aida fabric
thread
soft pencil
embroidery floss
vanishing fabric marker
6 x 6½-inch gingham
13-inch narrow white eyelet lace edging
1¾ yards of 4-inch-wide eyelet lace edging
6 x 7-inch piece of white backing fabric
polyester stuffing
potpourri
four buttons

1 Find the center of the Aida fabric by folding it in half each way and basting along the creases. Transfer your chosen initials to the fabric (see Steps 1 and 2 on page 31), and sew them in a cross-stitch so that one initial lies on each side of the central line.

2 Cut a 4-inch square of paper. Place this diagonally on the embroidery so that one corner lies on each basted line. Draw around it with a vanishing fabric marker and cut out the diamond shape.

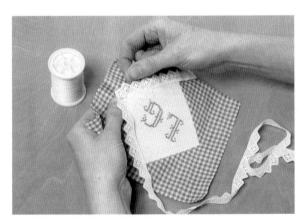

3 Pin and stitch the diamond shape to the center of the gingham. Slip-stitch the narrow eyelet lace around the diamond, mitering it neatly at the corners (see Techniques).

4 Join the wide eyelet lace to make a circle. Fold this into fourths, and mark the quarters with notches on the top edge. Make four lines of gathering stitches, by hand or machine, between the notches (see Techniques).

41

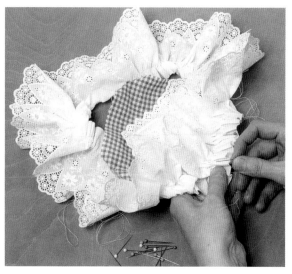

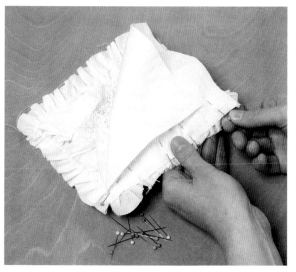

5 Pin one notch to each corner of the gingham so that the lace lies toward the center. Draw up the gathering threads so that the frill fits along each side, and knot the thread ends. Distribute the gathers evenly, allowing a little more fullness at each corner. Pin and baste in place.

6 Pin the gathers to the gingham, so that they do not get caught in the stitching. With right sides facing, pin the gingham front to the white backing fabric. Stitch them together ½ inch from the edge, leaving a 2-inch gap on one side.

7 Clip the corners and turn the cover right side out. Stuff with stuffing and potpourri, then slip-stitch the opening closed.

8 Finish by sewing a button onto each corner of the cushion with embroidery floss.

SILVER TOUCH

Silver machine-embroidery thread and glitzy metallic organza combine beautifully with gray velvet to make a luxurious cushion. Practice the fluid machine-embroidery on spare fabric before trying it out on the velvet. The hoop is important for holding the fabric taut and moving it around.

YOU WILL NEED
20 inches of 36-inch-wide gray velvet
vanishing fabric marker
embroidery hoop
silver machine-embroidery thread
8 inches of 36-inch-wide pleated metallic organza
thread
16-inch zipper
16-inch-square cushion pad

1 For the cushion front, cut a piece of velvet 17 inches square. Using the vanishing fabric marker, draw wavy guidelines for the embroidery. Place the fabric in the embroidery hoop. Select a free-embroidery or darning mode on the sewing machine and attach a darning foot. Stitch the design using the silver machine-embroidery thread.

2 Cut a strip of metallic organza measuring 67 x 2 inches, joining strips as necessary. With raw edges matching, fold the strip in half lengthwise, pin, baste and machine-stitch along the raw edges. For the cushion back, cut one piece of velvet measuring 17 x 14 inches and one piece measuring 17 x 4½ inches. Stitch the zipper in the seam with a ½-inch allowance.

3 Pin the organza frill around the embroidered cushion front, joining the ends as for piping (see Techniques). Machine-stitch. With right sides facing and the zipper open, pin the cushion front and back together. Stitch around the edge with a ½-inch seam allowance. Clip the corners and turn right side out. Insert the cushion pad and close the zipper.

ORGANZA DUO

A metallic-organza cover slipped over a satin cushion makes a theatrical combination.
When choosing the fabrics, hold the organza over the satin to see how the colors
affect one another when they are combined.

YOU WILL NEED
20 inches of 36-inch-wide satin
thread
Velcro
15-inch-square cushion pad
1 yard of 45-inch-wide metallic organza
tailor's chalk
ruler

1 For the front, cut a 16½-inch square of satin and for the back cut two 16½ x 9½-inch pieces. Turn, press and stitch a ½-inch double hem on one long edge of each back piece. Pin and stitch the cushion front and back together, with right sides facing and back pieces overlapping.

2 Clip the corners and turn right side out. On the opening edges of the back, mark and stitch pairs of press fasteners at even intervals. Insert the cushion pad and close the fasteners.

3 For the organza cover, cut one 20-inch square for the front and two 20 x 11-inch pieces for the back. Turn and press a double ½-inch hem on one long edge of each back piece. Assemble and stitch together as for the satin cover, with a ½-inch seam allowance.

4 Trim away the seam allowance to ¼ inch from the stitching, and clip the corners. Turn the cover right side out, and topstitch ¼ inch from the folded edge. On the cushion front, mark a line 2 inches from the edge all around, using tailor's chalk and a ruler. Machine-stitch along the line.

5 On the opening edges of the cover back, mark and stitch pairs of Velcro squares at intervals. Insert the satin cushion and fasten the organza cover.

Above: On this cushion, the pad is covered with bright satin and the impact is diffused by a second cover of translucent fabric.

HEARTS AND FLOWERS

A heart is a pleasing shape, whether for Valentine's Day or all year round. Go overboard with this one in silk and velvet, and trim it with an ornate silk rose. Make a whole selection of cushions and pile them up at the head of your bed for a touch of glamour.

YOU WILL NEED
heart-shaped cushion pad
graph paper
cardboard
20 inches of 45-inch-wide lilac silk douppioni
20 inches of 45-inch-wide green velvet
piping cord
matching thread
7-inch zipper
8-inch blue silk douppioni
tailor's chalk
self-covered button
button maker (optional)

1 To make a cardboard template, first press one half of the cushion pad onto a piece of graph paper and draw around the edge. Mark a line ¼ inch outside the first, and cut around this second line. Place the paper pattern on a folded piece of cardboard and draw around it. Cut out the template and open it.

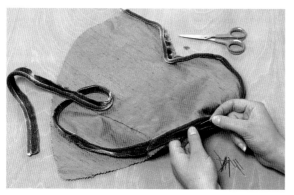

2 Cut out one heart in lilac silk and one in green velvet. Measure around one heart and cut a piece of piping cord to this measurement plus 2½ inches. Cut a 1½-inch-wide bias strip from green velvet and cover the piping cord, using a zipper foot. Pin the piping around the lilac silk cushion front, and stitch in place using a piping or a zipper foot.

3 With right sides facing, pin and machine-stitch the cushion front and back together with a ¼-inch seam, leaving a 7-inch gap in one straight edge for the zipper. Clip the seam allowance and turn the cover right side out. Hand-sew the zipper into the piped seam (see Techniques).

49

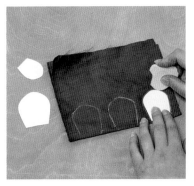

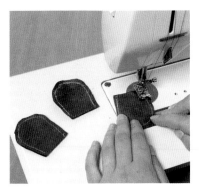

4 Draw a petal shape and enlarge it to three different sizes. Fold the blue silk douppioni in half and draw four large, five medium and four small petal shapes with the tailor's chalk. Carefully cut out the petals through the double layer of silk, adding ¼ inch all around.

5 Machine-stitch the petals in pairs along the marked lines, leaving the bottom edge of each unstitched. Turn the petals right side out and press.

6 Select a long stitch on the sewing machine. Stitch along the bottom edges of the largest petal shapes, then progress to the medium and lastly to the smallest petal shapes, without breaking off the thread in between. Secure the threads at one end and then, drawing on the top thread only, carefully pull up the gathers along the string of petals.

7 Arrange the petals, starting with the largest and spiraling the string around a central point. Pin in place. Stab-stitch to secure (see Techniques), and stitch to the top of the cushion front.

8 Draw around a self-covered button on the wrong side of some green velvet, adding a ¼-inch seam allowance. Cover the button using a button maker, or sew a running stitch around the edge of the velvet circle and pull up the thread to gather the fabric. Press the back of the button into place. Stitch the button to the center of the rose to cover the raw edges. Insert the cushion pad and close the zipper.

PINK PERFECTION

An extravagant patchwork of silk from the same color family makes this a luxury cushion. The edges are padded for added opulence. If pink is not your color, look for remnants of silk douppioni in jewel-bright colors such as jade, burnt orange or peacock blue.

YOU WILL NEED
paper
ruler
vanishing fabric marker
20 inches of 45-inch-wide silk douppioni each in red, lilac and pink
thread
polyester batting
Velcro
18-inch-square cushion pad

1 Cut a piece of paper 19 inches square for a template. Fold this in half diagonally and in half diagonally again, then unfold it and cut out the four triangles. Draw around these templates with vanishing fabric marker, and cut out four triangles in red silk and four in lilac. Pin one red and one lilac triangle together, with right sides facing. Machine-stitch along the two short edges with a ½-inch seam. Clip the seams. Assemble the other triangles in the same way. Turn right side out and press.

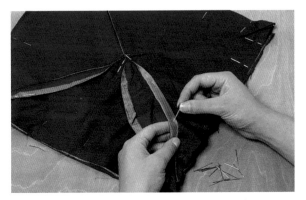

2 Cut a 19-inch-square pink silk cushion front. Place right side up on a table, and arrange the triangles with the lilac side facing down and with the unseamed edges matching the sides of the square. Pin in place. Pin the points of the triangles in place where they meet. Fold back the two shorter edges of the triangle to reveal the lilac side, and pin.

3 Topstitch the triangles to the cushion front ⅛ inch from the edge.

4 Cut a strip of batting measuring 2¼ yards x 2 inches, joining as necessary. Cut a 2¼-yard-long x 3-inch-wide bias strip of pink silk, and place it on a table, with the right side down. Roll up the batting and place it along the center of the strip. Pin the fabric evenly around the batting.

5 Machine-stitch along the strip to complete the piping, using a zipper foot. With raw edges matching, pin the piping all around the cushion front and then machine-stitch.

6 For the cushion back, cut two pieces of red silk measuring 19 x 12 inches. Turn and press a ¾-inch double hem on one long edge of each piece. Pin and machine-stitch in place. Place the cushion front and backs together with right sides facing and the back pieces overlapping. Pin and machine-stitch in place. Turn the cover right side out and sew a small piece of Velcro to the opening edges. Insert the cushion pad and then close the fastening.

GRAY SILK TRELLIS

The unusual fringing made from the main silk fabric is easy to sew, and yet looks really effective. Choose attractive buttons to hold the trelliswork in place and for fastening the rouleau loops on the back. Finish with a tassel at each corner, made from the same silk douppioni.

YOU WILL NEED

20 inches of 45-inch-wide gray silk douppioni

thread

23 shell buttons

blunt needle or safety pin

four ½-inch cotton balls

22 x 12-inch cushion pad

1 For the cushion front, cut a piece of gray silk measuring 23 x 13 inches. For the trelliswork, cut several strips of silk 1 inch wide. On each strip fold one long edge over by ½ inch, and topstitch ⅛ inch from the folded edge. Using a needle, carefully separate and remove the threads from both raw edges, pulling away the threads right up to the seam line to make a fringe.

2 Arrange the frayed strips on the cushion front in a lattice pattern, with the parallel strips placed 4½ inches apart.

3 Sew a button at each of the intersections, then stitch all around the edge of the fabric to hold the strips in position.

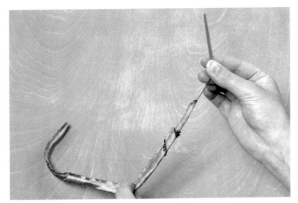

4 To make the rouleau loops, cut a strip of fabric measuring 13 x 1¼ inches. Fold in half lengthwise with right sides together, and machine-stitch ¼ inch from the folded edge. Attach a thread to one end and pass the strip through the eye of a blunt needle or a safety pin, then push the needle or safety pin through the tube to turn the loop right side out. Cut the strip into three 4¼-inch lengths. For the cushion back, cut one piece of fabric measuring 8 x 13 inches and one piece measuring 20 x 13 inches.

5 On the smaller back piece, turn and press a ¾-inch-wide double hem on one long edge. On one short edge of the larger piece, position and pin the three rouleau loops, checking that the loops will fit over the buttons. Baste and machine-stitch the loops in place. Cut a lining measuring 13 x 2 inches, and neaten one long edge. With right sides together, pin and machine-stitch the facing over the rouleau loops. Turn and press the facing to the wrong side and then topstitch.

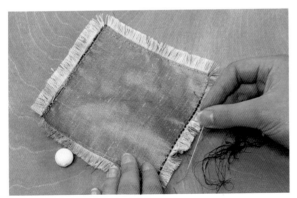

6 With right sides facing and raw edges matching, place the larger back piece on the front piece. Place the smaller back piece on top, with the right side facing down and raw edges matching. Sew the cover around all four sides and turn through. Sew on buttons to match the loops. For each tassel, cut two pieces of fabric 4 inches square. Work a zigzag stitch ¼ inch from the raw edges. Fray the edges (see Step 1), pulling away threads up to the stitched line.

7 Mark a 2-inch-diameter circle in the center of the square. Run a gathering thread along the marked line. Place a cotton ball in the center, draw up the gathers and secure them, then wind the thread around the gathering thread and secure with a stitch. Insert the needle inside the cotton ball and bring it out at the top of the tassel, then stitch to one corner of the cushion. Repeat to make three more tassels. Insert the cushion pad and fasten the rouleau loops.

STITCH IN TIME

These two stylish covers are both suitable for beginners to tackle. The dark wool square is simply embroidered with three rows of running stitch around the edge. The white cord trim and toggle fastenings on both cushions add to their homespun appeal.

EMBROIDERED CUSHION

YOU WILL NEED
20 inches of 45-inch-wide gray wool fabric
white perle embroidery floss
embroidery needle
thread
pinking shears
2¼ yards white cord
three toggles
18-inch-square cushion pad
vanishing fabric marker

1 For the cushion front, cut a 19-inch square of fabric. Mark a line 3 inches from the edge all around. Work a running stitch in embroidery floss along the marked line, then work two more parallel lines ½ inch apart inside the marked line.

2 For the cushion back, use pinking shears to cut one piece of fabric measuring 7 x 19 inches and another measuring 17½ x 19 inches. Neaten the opening edges and turn under by 2 inches. Pin, and machine-stitch ⅛ inch and then ¾ inch from the folded edge. Work three rows of running stitch in embroidery floss along both edges.

3 Assemble the cushion front and backs with right sides facing and the back pieces overlapping. Pin and machine-stitch around the edge with a ½-inch seam and leaving a 4-inch gap in one side. Clip the corners, turn right side out and press. Push one end of the cord into the opening in the seam, and stab-stitch in place along the seam (see Techniques).

4 At each corner of the cover, carefully twist the cord into a small loop, then continue along the next seam.

5 Push the other end of the cord into the opening in the seam, overlapping the two ends slightly. Stab-stitch in place and slip-stitch the opening closed.

6 Mark the positions of three toggles at equal distances on the underside of the cushion back. Mark the corresponding positions for the loops on the overlap, using a vanishing fabric marker. At the edge of the overlap work three or four large stitches over one finger in embroidery floss, in each marked position, ensuring that these threads will fit easily over the toggles.

7 Work a tight blanket stitch along the threads to hold them together (see Techniques). Make a small stitch in the fabric to finish off. Stitch the toggles in place and insert the cushion pad.

FRINGED CUSHION

YOU WILL NEED
8 inches of wool fabric each in green,
burgundy and red
12 inches of gray-blue wool fabric
pinking shears
sewing thread
pink embroidery floss
embroidery needle
four toggles
16-inch-square cushion pad

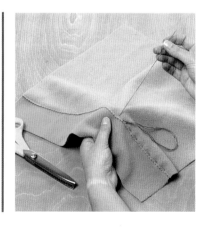

1 For the cushion back, cut one piece of green fabric measuring 5¼ x 17 inches and one piece of gray-blue fabric measuring 13 x 17 inches, using pinking shears. Lap the gray-blue fabric over the green by 1¼ inches, and topstitch 1½ inches from the pinked edge. Using pink embroidery floss, work a line of running stitch along the machine-stitched line.

2 To make a pinked fringe, cut two 67-inch fabric strips, one in burgundy 1¼ inches wide and one in green 1½ inches wide. Place the strips together, matching one long edge of each, and then pin and machine-stitch down the center. Trim the long edges of the burgundy fabric to ½ inch and the green to ½ inch from the stitched line.

3 Arrange the fringing around the right side of the cushion back. Pin and machine-stitch in place. For the cushion front, cut a piece of red fabric measuring 5¼ x 17 inches, a piece of burgundy fabric measuring 8 x 17 inches and a piece of gray-blue fabric measuring 10 x 17 inches.

4 Attach the red and burgundy pieces by their longest edges. Neaten the opening edges of the front pieces and fold under by 2 inches. Pin and machine-stitch ¼ inch from the folded edge. Work a running stitch with pink embroidery floss along the machine-stitched line.

5 Assemble the cushion pieces with right sides together and overlapping the gray-blue underside piece. Pin and machine-stitch together with a ½-inch seam. Clip the corners and turn right side out. On the underlap, mark the toggle positions. On the overlap, mark the positions of the loops. Make four loops as in Step 6 of the Embroidered Cushion. Insert the cushion pad and fasten the toggles.

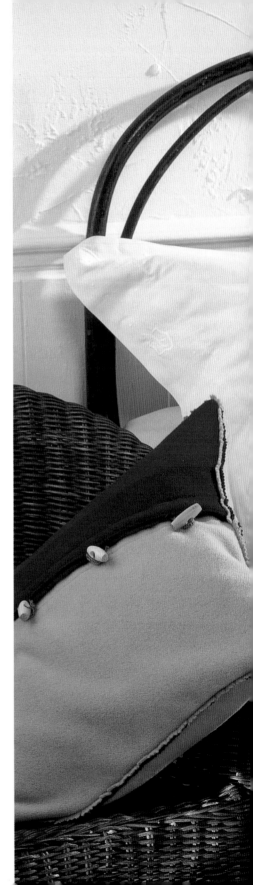

RIBBON WEAVING

Ribbons come in such a wonderful array of colors, widths and textures that you can thoroughly indulge yourself by making this cushion. Only short lengths of ribbon are needed, so add end-of-roll bargains to your own workbasket collection to make up the amount needed.

YOU WILL NEED
20 inches of 36-inch-wide calico
20 inches satin
thread
16-inch zipper
fusible bonding web
selection of ribbons
2 yards piping cord
16-inch-square cushion pad

1 For the cushion front, cut a piece of calico 17 inches square. For the back, cut two pieces of satin measuring 17 x 9½ inches. Attach the two back pieces, inserting a zipper in the seam. Cut a piece of fusible bonding web 17 inches square and press face down on the calico. Peel away the backing paper from the bonding web.

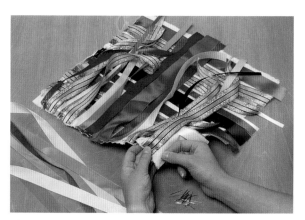

2 Cut the ribbons into 17-inch lengths. Pin the ribbons to two adjacent sides of the calico, ½ inch from the edges.

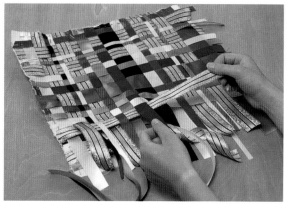

3 Weave the horizontal ribbons over and under the vertical ribbons, pulling them taut. Pin them in place at the other end.

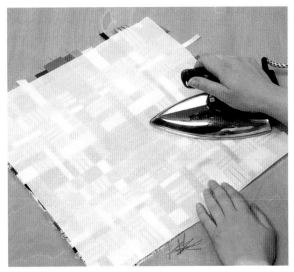

4 Turn the calico over and, using a hot iron, press the calico to fuse the woven ribbons in place.

5 To make the ruched piping to go around the edges of the cushion, cut 1½-inch-wide bias strips of satin to twice the length of the piping cord, attaching the strips as necessary.

6 Fold the bias binding in half around the piping cord, and pin. Secure the cord at one end, then machine-stitch along it for 12 inches. Raise the foot, leaving the needle in the fabric. Pull the cord through the fabric tube to gather the fabric. Repeat along the length of the piping and secure at the end.

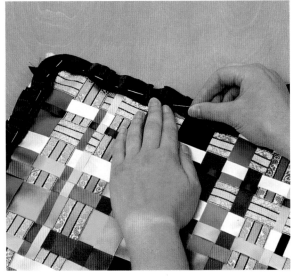

7 Pin the ruched piping around the cushion front, and stitch. Place the cushion back on top, and pin into position. With right sides facing and the zipper open, machine-stitch all around the seam. Clip the corners and turn the cover right side out. Insert the cushion pad and close the zipper.

COUNTRY CHECK

Patchwork and gingham go together like strawberries and cream. The patchwork front is machine-stitched for speed and strength, then hand-finished with traditional quilting knots. The cover is completed with simple ties to fasten the back.

YOU WILL NEED

cardboard

selection of gingham fabrics

thread

string

pushpin

pencil

paper

20 inches of 45-inch-wide calico

tapestry needle

white perle embroidery floss

16-inch-diameter cushion pad

1 Make a cardboard template 4½ inches square. Draw around the template on the gingham fabric and add a ½-inch seam allowance. Cut out 16 squares. Pin these together in pairs, with right sides facing. Stitch along one edge with a ½-inch seam allowance. Attach the pairs and make strips of four squares. Press the seams open.

2 Attach two strips along one long edge, taking care to match the seams.

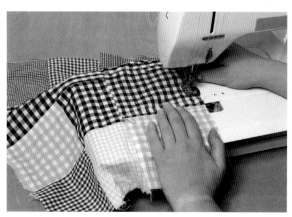

3 Continue adding the strips to form a large square. Press the seams open.

65

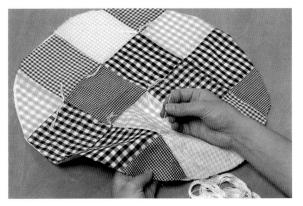

4 Using the string, pushpin and pencil, draw a 17-inch-diameter circle on paper. Cut this out, and use it to cut a circle of calico and a circle of patchwork for the cushion front. Place the patched piece wrong side down on the calico. Baste around the edge to hold the two layers together.

5 Thread the tapestry needle with several lengths of embroidery floss. Insert the needle at the corners of the patches, leaving an end of 1½ inches. Make a stitch and bring the needle back through to the right side of the fabric.

6 Tie the strands in a knot and trim. Remove the basting thread. For the cushion back, fold the paper template vertically into fourths. Cut along one fold line to make one large and one small template. Cut the two back pieces from calico, adding 1 inch to each straight edge. Cut two facings 2 inches wide and neaten one long edge of each. Pin one facing to the smaller back piece, with right sides facing. Stitch the seam, turn and press. Stitch a hem, ⅛ inch and ¾ inch from the seamed edge.

7 Make six ties from 4 x 7-inch pieces of gingham (see Techniques). Position three ties at equal intervals along the opening edge of the larger back piece, matching the raw edges, and machine-stitch. Pin the second facing to the opening edge, over the ties and with right sides facing, and machine-stitch. Turn and fold the facing to the wrong side. Machine-stitch the hem, as in Step 6.

8 On the back underlap, mark the corresponding positions of the other three ties. Turn under the raw edge of each remaining tie and pin in place. Topstitch in an "X" pattern. Pin the cushion front to the backs with right sides facing, and machine-stitch around the edge with a ½-inch seam. Clip the seam allowances all around. Turn right side out, insert the cushion pad and fasten the ties.

NATURAL CUSHIONS

Each of these natural finishes brings a touch of individuality to purchased, ready-made cushion covers, with a minimal outlay of effort and expense. Display one cushion on its own, or pile all three together on one chair for a comfortable, homespun look.

YOU WILL NEED
natural-colored cushion covers
thread

SEASHELL BORDER
old shell necklace
larger seashells
drill and ⅛₆-inch high-speed
steel drill bit

SOFT-CORD APPLIQUÉ
¼-inch natural cotton piping cord
small safety pins

ROSE APPLIQUÉ WITH RAFFIA TASSELS
raffia
builder's brick line
sisal rope
buttons (optional)

SEASHELL BORDER

1 Remove the shells from the necklace string. Place the larger shells on a firm surface, and very carefully drill a hole in each.

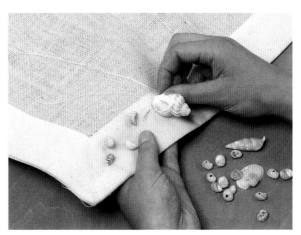

2 Stitch the shells randomly in place around the border of the cushion, taking care to secure with additional backstitches every few shells.

68

SOFT-CORD APPLIQUÉ

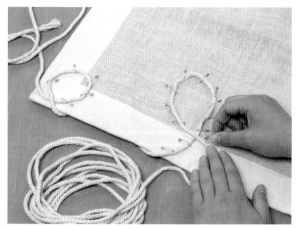

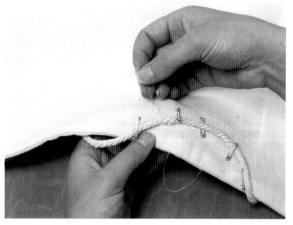

1 Drape the piping cord over the cushion cover, letting it fall naturally into curves and curlicues. Secure with safety pins. Let the cord travel across the reverse, as well as the face, of the cover for a flowing, naturalistic effect. Knot the loose ends together and tie each off in a simple knot.

2 Slip-stitch the cord securely in place, using small stitches that pass through, rather than over, the entire surface of the cord. Remove the safety pins.

ROSE APPLIQUÉ WITH RAFFIA TASSELS

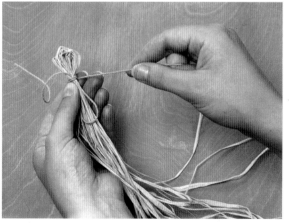

1 To make a raffia tassel, first loop approximately 15 strands of raffia around your hand.

2 Place the builder's brick line in a loop at the top end of the raffia, with the loop pointing downward. Begin whipping the line around itself, starting at the looped end of the raffia (which will become the head of the tassel) and working down toward the skirt. ▶

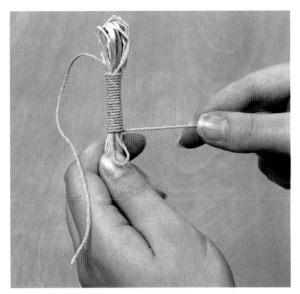

3 Continue wrapping the line evenly and tightly around the raffia until you reach the end of the loop of brick line.

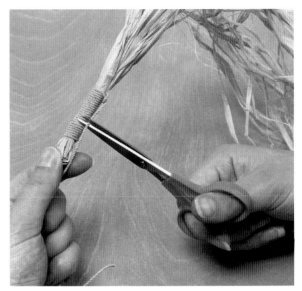

4 Pass the working end of the brick line through the loop. Cut the end so that it is approximately ¼ inch long.

5 Gently pull the brick line at the head of the tassel to pull through the other cut end, then work both ends securely into the neck binding. Make three more tassels in the same way.

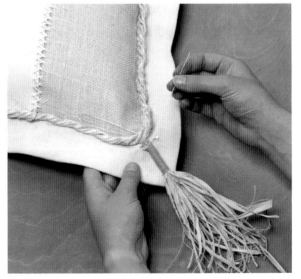

6 Stitch the sisal rope in place around the border of the cushion cover. Slip-stitch a tassel to each corner of the cover, and trim the ends of the raffia skirts to the desired length. Embellish the cover even more by sewing on buttons, if desired.

BEAUTIFUL BATIK

The technique of batik, which originated in Java, involves making designs on fabric by waxing parts not to be dyed. This cushion cover uses four different-colored dyes to build up the rich pattern. The batik materials are widely available at crafts suppliers.

YOU WILL NEED
32 inches of 36-inch-wide white cotton fabric
washing soda
paper
black felt-tip pen
pencil
9 ounces batik wax
double boiler
adjustable tapestry frame
pushpins
tjanting for applying the wax
paper towels
old paintbrush
bucket
urea
procion 'm' dyes in chrome yellow, turquoise,
peacock blue and navy
salt
rubber gloves
thread
Velcro
12-inch-square cushion pad

1 Wash the fabric thoroughly, and soak it in a solution of washing soda overnight to remove all traces of fabric finish. Rinse and let dry. Cut one 18½-inch square and two 18½ x 12-inch rectangles of fabric. Draw out the design from the back of the book onto a 16-inch square of paper and go over the lines with a felt-tip pen. Trace the design onto the center of the fabric with a pencil.

2 Heat the wax to between 122°F and 140°F in the double boiler. Stretch the fabric square onto the tapestry frame with pins. Using a tjanting, begin to wax the areas you want to remain white (the wax must penetrate the fabric so that it looks wet). Use a pad of paper towels to prevent drips.

3 For larger areas of the design, carefully outline them with the tjanting first and then fill them in using the old paintbrush.

4 Once all the white areas have been waxed, turn the frame over and, if necessary, rewax any areas where the wax has not penetrated completely. Let dry thoroughly. Next, prepare a yellow dye bath (see below). Add the batik square and the two rectangles to the bucket, and stir continuously for six minutes. Dissolve 1 tablespoon of soda in a little warm water and add this to the bucket. Let the fabric soak for 45 more minutes, stirring occasionally. Remove the fabric and rinse it in cold water until the water runs clear, then hang it out to dry. Once dry, wax the areas that are to stay yellow.

5 Prepare a turquoise dye bath and immerse the fabric for 45 minutes. Once rinsed and dry, wax the areas that are to remain green. Prepare a peacock-blue dye bath using 2 teaspoons of dye this time, and leave the fabric in the dye bath for up to an hour. Once the fabric is rinsed and dry, wax the areas that are to remain blue-green. Plunge the fabric into very cold water to "crack" some of the large areas of wax. Prepare a dye bath using 1 tablespoon of navy dye. Let the fabric soak for several hours, then rinse and let dry.

PREPARING THE YELLOW CHROME DYE
Half fill a bucket with cold water. Dissolve 2 tablespoons of urea in 1 pint of lukewarm water. In a separate container mix 1 teaspoon of chrome yellow dye to a paste. Stir the urea solution into the dye paste and pour into the bucket. Dissolve 4 tablespoons salt in 1 pint of lukewarm water and add to the bucket.

TIP Wear rubber gloves throughout the dyeing process in order to prevent the wax and dye from harming your hands.

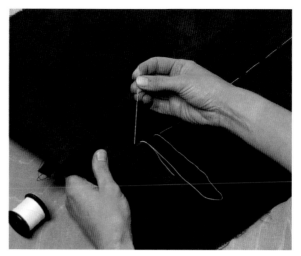

6 Protect your ironing board with an old sheet or cover. Place the batik between several layers of newspaper, and iron over it to melt the wax. Keep replacing the paper until most of the wax has been removed. The last traces of wax can be removed by dry cleaning or by immersing the fabric in boiling water. Press all the pieces while they are still damp.

7 Stitch a small hem along the long edge of each rectangle of fabric. Overlap the hems to make an 18½-inch square with right sides facing up, then pin and baste together.

8 With right sides facing, pin the front and back of the cushion together. Stitch around the outside edge of the batik. Trim the seams, clip the corners and turn right side out. Remove the basting thread.

9 Ease out the corners and press the seams. Pin and stitch close to the inside edge of the border, and trim the threads. Sew a small piece of Velcro to the opening edges of the cover. Insert the pad and close the Velcro.

IN THE ROUND

A luxurious velvet bolster looks good on a window seat or adorning a chaise-longue. Use up leftover furnishing fabrics to make this simple patchwork cushion formed from strips. Trim the gathered ends with self-covered buttons, or add tassels to finish if you prefer.

YOU WILL NEED
18-inch-long bolster cushion pad
pinking shears
remnants of velvet in orange, light green, dark green and lilac
thread
vanishing fabric marker
two self-covered buttons
button maker (optional)

1 Measure the circumference of the bolster pad. Using pinking shears, cut one piece of orange velvet 8¼ inches wide, two pieces each of light green 3 inches wide, dark green 4 inches wide, and lilac 6½ inches wide by the circumference plus 1¼ inches. Pin and machine-stitch the strips together by the longest edges as shown.

2 Fold the patched piece in half horizontally with right sides facing and the raw edges matching. Pin and machine-stitch the seam to form a tube. Turn the cover right side out.

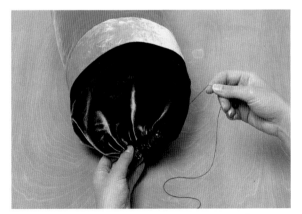

3 Place the cushion pad inside the cover. Using a double thread, run a gathering thread around each end. Draw up the thread, tuck the raw edges inside and stitch to secure.

4 Using the vanishing fabric marker, draw around both of the self-covered buttons on the wrong side of a piece of light green velvet, adding a ¼-inch seam allowance. Cut out the circles.

5 Cover each button using a button maker, or simply sew a running stitch around the edge of each circle and pull up the thread to gather the fabric. Press the backs of the buttons into place.

6 Stitch a covered button over the gathered edge at each end of the bolster.

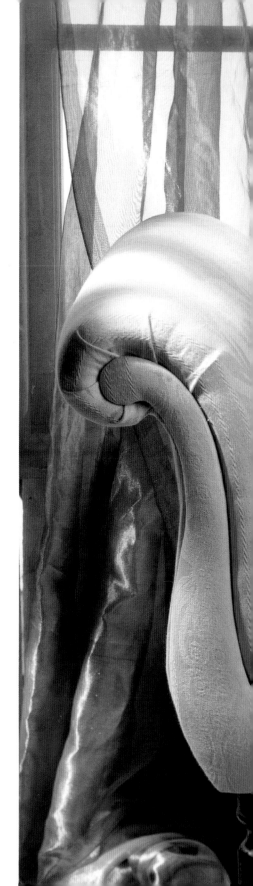

Above: This simple bolster cushion was made from a single piece of velvet and trimmed with wide ribbon. The inner section is lined with a different color fabric, and the ends simply gathered around the cushion pad and then wrapped with cord.

MATERIALS

As well as the fabric for your cushion, you will need to choose thread, a type of fastening and trimmings or other decorations. Some of the most commonly used cushion materials are listed here.

BATTING
This synthetic padding can be used for padding piping or for making cushion pads.

BIAS BINDING
Buy this ready-made or make your own. Cut on the bias (or cross) to give stretch, these strips may be used to make piping and rouleau loops.

BRAID
This woven ribbon is used for trimming and is available in many colors, weights and widths.

BUTTONS
Available in many colors and weights, buttons can be used both decoratively, as part of a design, and to close a cushion.

COTTON BALLS
Available at crafts stores, these are used to shape fabric tassels.

EMBROIDERY FLOSS
Available as perle, soft cotton and stranded, use this for embroidery and for making tassels.

EYELETS
Purchased in kit form along with a special fixing tool, eyelets can be used on their own or threaded with cord, ribbon or rope.

FRINGING
An edging made from cut threads, fringing is used to trim cushions.

FUSIBLE BONDING WEB
This is used to bond appliqué motifs to fabric prior to stitching, or to bond woven ribbons to a backing fabric.

MACHINE-EMBROIDERY THREAD
This thread is more lustrous than regular thread. It is also available in metallic shades.

PIPING CORD
This cotton cord can be covered with bias binding and inserted in seams. Ready-made piping can be bought in a limited range of colors.

RIBBON
Ribbon is available in a range of colors, widths and textures. Keep a collection of small pieces of ribbon handy for trimming cushions.

SELF-COVERED BUTTONS
Available in kit form and in a range of sizes, these may be used as decorative features – such as flower centers – or as closures.

TAPESTRY WOOLS
Hand-sew wool to the edges of cushions to add definition.

THREAD
Choose a slightly darker shade of thread when matching the fabric color. Thread should be of a similar fiber to that of the fabric being used: for example, cotton thread for cotton fabrics.

VELCRO PADS
These metallic fasteners are used for closing light weight fabric cushions. Press-fastener tape is also available, and is quicker to apply than individual fasteners.

VELCRO TAPE
This easy-to-use fastener simply presses together. It can be bought in strips or as small pads.

ZIPPERS
Available in many weights, lengths and colors, zippers come with either plastic or metal teeth.

Opposite clockwise from top left: piping cord, self-covered buttons, fusible bonding web, machine-embroidery thread, beads, ribbons, braid, shells, zipper, batting, embroidery floss, press-fastener tape, raffia, fringing, press-and-close fastening, eyelets and cotton balls.

TOOLS AND EQUIPMENT

For all the cushions in this book you will need a sewing machine and a basic sewing kit, which includes needles and pins, scissors and a tape measure. You will also need an iron for pressing seams, fusing appliqué and setting fabric paints. Some of the most useful tools for cushion-making are listed here. Each project also lists any special equipment you will need to make the cushion.

COMPASS
Use this for drawing circles. If you do not have a compass, draw around cups for small circles; to draw larger circles use plates.

CORNER TURNER
This tool is useful for turning points and corners of cushions.

EMBROIDERY HOOP
This consists of two hoops that fit snugly inside each other. Made of wood or plastic with a spring closure, it is used for both hand and machine embroidery.

FABRIC DYES
Hot and cold dyes are available. Fabrics with natural fibers, such as cotton and linen, can be dyed most successfully.

FABRIC PAINTS
There is a wide range of easy-to-use products. Choose water-based paints that can be set with an iron. The paints can be mixed and applied with a brush to create an unlimited number of colors.

GAUGE
An ideal tool for marking hems and borders, this has a marker that can be set to a fixed measurement.

IRON
A heavy iron with both steam and spray functions is ideal.

MACHINE NEEDLES AND NEEDLES
Choose a needle that is right for the weight of fabric. Most cottons and upholstery fabrics require a 80/12 or 90/14 needle. Choose needles with large eyes when using tapestry yarn.

PINKING SHEARS
To prevent seam allowances from fraying, use pinking shears to cut the pieces or to trim the seams.

PINS
Fine dressmaking pins are ideal, as they will not mark fabric.

RULER
You will need a wooden or metal ruler for drafting templates.

SCISSORS
For embroidery and for clipping seams, use scissors with 3½–4-inch blades. For cutting out fabrics, use heavier scissors with 8–9-inch blades.

SEAM RIPPER
Use this to remove basting thread and to unpick any mistakes.

SEWING MACHINE
You will need a basic sewing machine with straight and zigzag stitches, as well as a zipper and piping foot, and a darning foot for machine embroidery.

T-SQUARE
Use a T-square to find the bias in fabric and for drafting templates.

TAPE MEASURE
Buy a non-stretch tape measure.

VANISHING FABRIC MARKER
The marks fade on exposure to air. You could also use tailor's chalk, or a soft pencil on heavier fabrics.

Opposite clockwise from top left: embroidery hoop, thread, fabric dyes, tape measure, gauge, needles, seam ripper, soft pencil, vanishing fabric marker, corner turner, sewing machine, pins, scissors, paper for drawing templates on, T-square, fabric paints, iron and safety pins.

TECHNIQUES

The needlework techniques used in making, fastening and embellishing cushions are easy to learn and, once mastered, will be used over and over. As well as some basic stitches, you will need to know how to sew on zippers, piping and ribbons, stitch buttonholes and clip curves and corners.

STITCHES

BLANKET STITCH

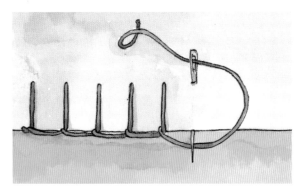

Insert the needle ⅜ inch from the edge of the fabric. Loop the thread under the point of the needle, pull the needle through and insert it again, ½ inch to the right of the first stitch. Continue in this way along the edge of the fabric.

STAB STITCH

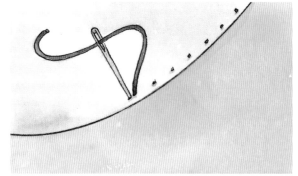

Bring the needle up through the fabric from the underside and down again almost in the same place to catch a small amount of fabric. This stitch should be almost invisible on the right side, and is mostly used to hold layers of fabric or cord in place.

GATHERING STITCH

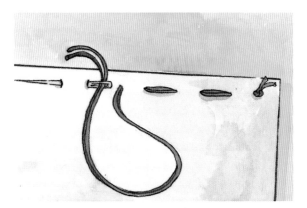

Double the thread, tie a knot in one end and sew a running stitch. Draw up the thread to form gathers.

SLIP STITCH

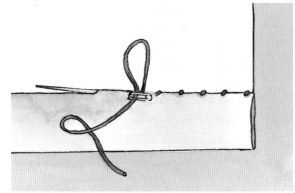

This is used to hold hems in place or to close gaps invisibly. Pick up only a few threads at a time.

BASIC TECHNIQUES

APPLIQUÉ USING FUSIBLE BONDING WEB

 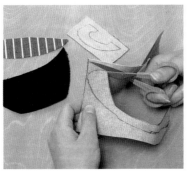 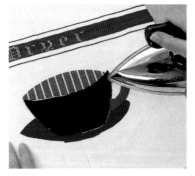

1 Enlarge the design and trace it onto the backing paper of the fusible web. Place the sticky (fusible) side face down on the wrong side of the appliqué fabric. Fuse in place with a hot iron.

2 Cut out the motif around the marked line and carefully peel away the backing paper.

3 Place the motif sticky side down on the main fabric and press with a hot iron.

MAKING BIAS BINDING

1 Cut a rectangular piece of fabric twice as long as it is wide. Hold a set square against the selvage, or fold the fabric diagonally to find the bias. Mark this fold with pins. From this fold draw parallel lines 1½ inches apart, marking as many strips as necessary using tailor's chalk and a ruler. Carefully trim away the triangular corners.

2 Pin the short edges together so that the end of one strip extends beyond the seam at the top and bottom. Stitch a ¼-inch seam and press open.

3 Cut along the marked lines to make one continuous length of bias binding.

APPLYING PIPING

1 Measure around the front of the cushion cover and cut a piece of cord and bias binding to this length plus 2½ inches. Fold in half lengthwise and pin the fabric around the cord. Baste and machine-stitch with a piping or a zipper foot.

2 Starting at an unobtrusive point, pin the cord all around the cushion front with the cord facing inward and the raw edges matching. Baste and then machine-stitch all the way around, using a piping or a zipper foot. Clip the seam allowance at the curves and corners.

3 To join the piping cord, unpick ¾ inch of the machine stitching from the beginning of the piping. Trim away the encased piping cord so that the two cords abut, and lap one end of the casing over the other, turning under the raw edge. Pin in place and machine-stitch. Slip-stitch to secure.

CLIPPING CURVES AND CORNERS

To allow a curved seam or a hem to lie flat, it is helpful to snip the seam allowances. Cut out small triangular shapes along the edge, taking care not to snip through the stitching. To clip corners, cut straight across the corner, as near to the stitching as possible.

MITERING RIBBON

1 Starting at one corner, pin both edges of the ribbon parallel to the hem, making folds in the corner. Machine-stitch all around to attach the ribbon to the fabric, and tuck the excess ribbon under at the corners to form a neat diagonal seam.

2 Next, ladder-stitch the seam together. This is done by simply making horizontal stitches between the folds and running the needle through the fold.

CUSHION CLOSURES

BUTTONS AND BUTTONHOLES

Press a double hem twice the width of the button on both opening edges. Machine-stitch the hems. Mark the button positions on the underlap and buttonholes on the overlap at even intervals, making sure that the marks match. Make each buttonhole length one-and-a-half times the width of the button. At the marked points, stitch the buttons in place: Place a matchstick on the button and work a few stitches through the holes in the button; remove the matchstick and wind the thread around the shank. At the marked positions, work a close zigzag stitch along the buttonhole. At the end mark, select a wider stitch and work a bar of six stitches. Reset the stitch and zigzag back along the marked edge. Work another bar at this end, and back stitch to secure. Using sharp embroidery scissors or a seam ripper, snip between the edges to make a slit.

ROULEAU LOOPS

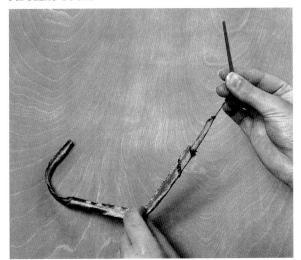

1 Cut a 1¼-inch-wide bias strip of fabric. Fold it lengthwise with right sides together, and machine stitch ¼ inch from the edge. Pass the end through a tapestry needle or onto a safety pin, and push through the tube to turn it right side out.

2 Pin the rouleau loops on the right side of the opening edges of the cushion cover, spacing them evenly. They should fit easily over the buttons. Baste and machine-stitch the loops in place. With right sides together, pin the facing over the rouleau loops and machine-stitch the seam. Turn and press the facing to the wrong side, and topstitch.

BUTTON LOOPS

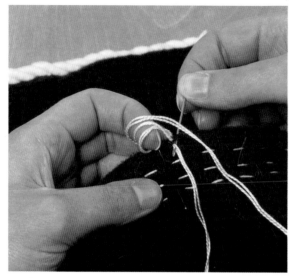

At the marked points on the folded edge, work several stitches back and forth over your finger, checking that the stitches fit comfortably over the button. Starting at one end of the stitches, work over the strands with a close blanket stitch.

FABRIC TIES

Cut 7 x 4-inch pairs of ties. Fold them in half length-wise and stitch one short and one long side, then clip the corners and turn right side out. Mark the positions of the ties on the right side of the opening edges of the cushion cover, making sure that they match up. Pin the ties facing inward with raw edges matching. With right sides together, pin the facing over the ties, matching raw edges, and then machine-stitch the seam.

ZIPPERS

1 Mark the position of the zipper along the seam. Machine-stitch or baste the seam in which the zipper is to be fitted, using large stitches (these are removed later). Press the seam allowance open.

2 Baste the zipper to the wrong side of the seam, ensuring that the zipper is centered over the seam. Using a zipper foot, topstitch along each side of the zipper and across each end.

INSERTING A ZIPPER IN A PIPED SEAM

Place the zipper face down on the piped seam, lining up the piping stitching with the teeth of the zipper. Pin, baste and hand-sew or machine-stitch ¼ inch from the teeth. Press under the seam allowance of the other opening edge. Pin and baste the folded edge to the zipper so that the edge meets the piping neatly. Hand-sew or machine-stitch ¼ inch from the folded edge and across each end of the zipper.

ATTACHING VELCRO

Turn and press a double hem the width of the press-and-close fastening on each piece of fabric where the opening should be. Place one half of the Velcro on each hem, and machine-stitch the hem and fastening in place on each half.

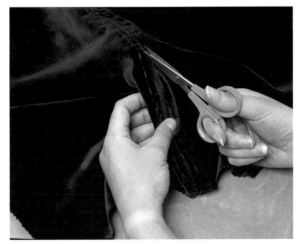

3 Using a seam ripper or small, sharp scissors, very carefully unpick the temporary basting stitches.

ATTACHING VELCRO

Turn, press and machine-stitch a double hem. Stitch the two halves of each piece of Velcro – one on each side of the closure – ensuring that pairs match up. Topstitch an "X" at each end of the closure, through both hems.

TEMPLATES

The templates given here are reproduced at the size they are used in the projects unless the measurements appear alongside the template. These templates should be enlarged using a photocopier.

Embroidered Heart, pp. 8–11

Flower Power, pp. 25–27

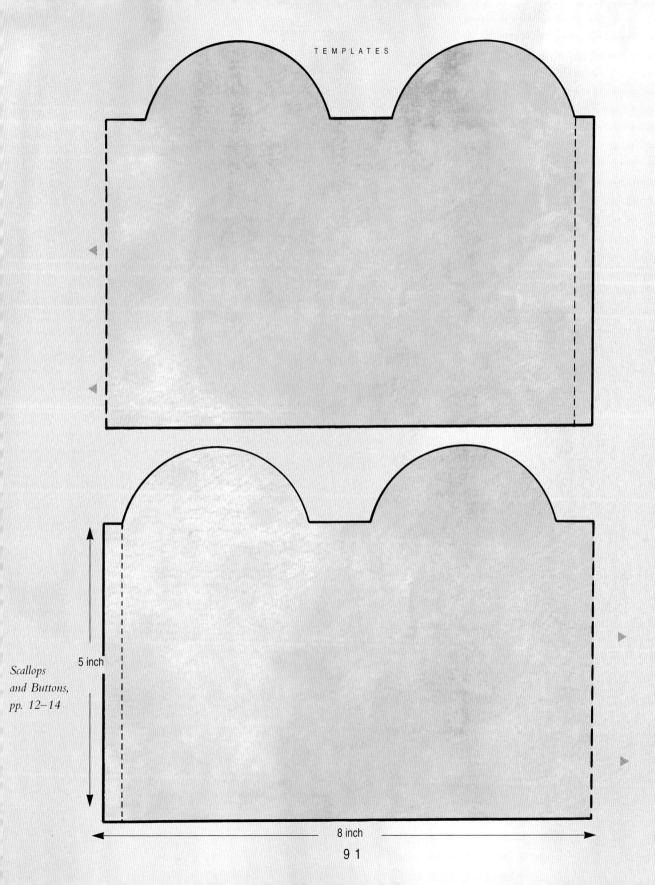

*Scallops
and Buttons,
pp. 12–14*

5 inch

8 inch

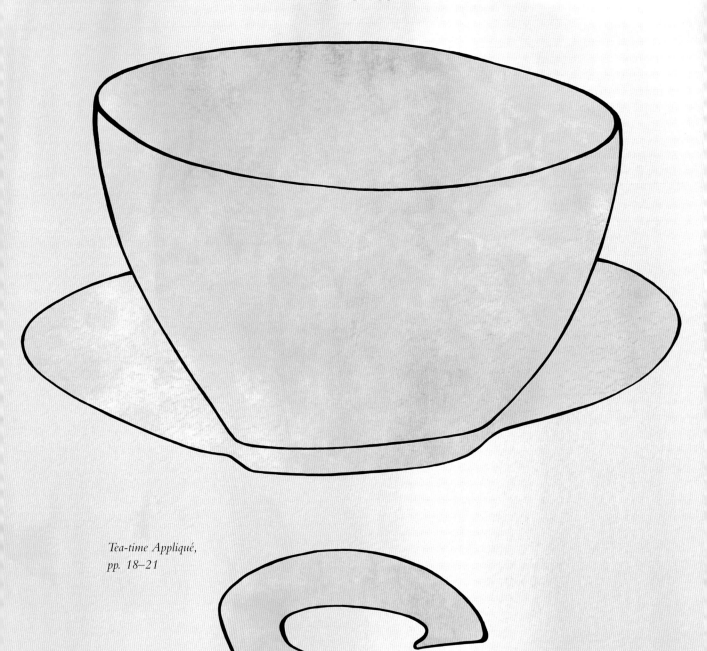

Tea-time Appliqué,
pp. 18–21

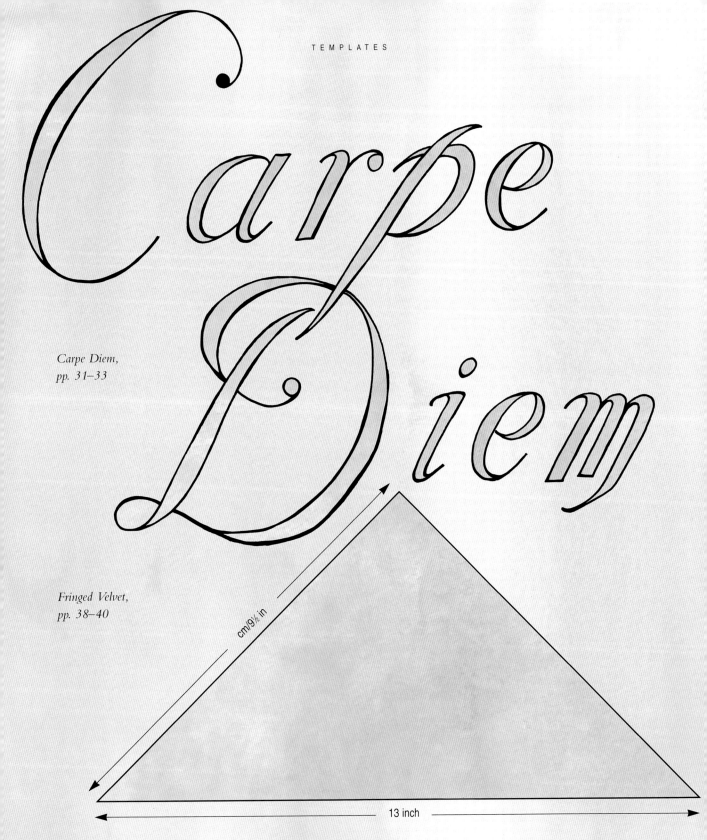

Carpe Diem

Carpe Diem,
pp. 31–33

Fringed Velvet,
pp. 38–40

cm/9½ in

13 inch

16 inch

inch

Beautiful Batik, pp. 72–75

94

ACKNOWLEDGMENTS

The publishers would like to thank the following people for designing the projects in this book: Isabel Stanley for the Fringed Velvet, pp. 38–40, Silver Touch, pp. 44–5, Organza Duo, pp. 46–8, Hearts and Flowers, pp. 49–51, Pink Perfection, pp. 52–4, Grey Silk Trellis, pp. 55–7, Stitch in Time, pp. 58–61, Ribbon Weaving, pp. 62–4, Country Check, pp. 65–7 and In the Round, pp. 76–9; Petra Boase for the Embroidered Heart, pp. 8–11, Scallops and Buttons, pp. 12–14, Going Dotty, pp. 15–17, Tea-time Appliqué, pp. 18–21 and Flower Power, pp. 25–7; Dorothy Wood for the Nautical Note, pp. 22–4, Take a Seat, pp. 34–7 and Beautiful Batik, pp. 72–5; Lucinda Ganderton for the Patchwork Velvet Pincushion, pp. 28–30 and Personally Yours, pp. 41–3; Deena Beverly for Carpe Diem, pp. 31–3 and Natural Cushions, pp. 68–71.

INDEX